POEMS

and

REFLECTIONS

on

LIFE

and

LOVE

by

RUDY PAKIZ

Singing River Publications, Inc.

Ely, Minnesota

Poems and Reflections on Life and Love

Layout:

Charles Morello, Jr.
IRIS Enterprises
Eveleth, MN

Published by:

Singing River Publications, Inc.
P. O. Box 72
Ely, MN, 55731 USA
www.singingriverpublications.com

Printed in Canada

50th Anniversary Card (Form OF003) reprinted by permission of Barton-Cotton, Inc, Baltimore, MD.

Photo on Rear Cover by Frances Bizal, Chisholm, MN

ISBN: 0-9759953-5-9

1. Memoir; 2. Christian Spirituality; 3. Christian Reflections

Table of Contents

Poetry in Part One

Poetry in Part Two

Pictures in Part One

Pictures in Part Two

Father Rudy Pakiz

INTRODUCTION

As a parish priest nearing retirement age I put together some of my poems with the two small booklets, "Simple Rhymes" (1991) and "Selected Poems" (1996) and passed them on to relatives and friends. The response was so gratifying that I was encouraged to do more writing.

Now that I am in my eighties, I feel it is time to combine all my poems into one volume and include some thoughts and experiences that shaped my faith and my life. Perhaps someone could learn from my observations and reflections as I have learned from others. As Jim Shannon, a classmate from our seminary days, said of my "Simple Rhymes", "They have brightened my days and enriched my prayers."

In Part One I will reflect on my personal story and focus on the loves that have moved me toward the Good, the True and the Beautiful. Some of the attractions that moved me were love of nature, love of people, love of God and love of life itself.

In Part Two I will include the poems that I think are worth preserving and may be of interest to others. My style of writing has already been expressed in one of my booklets as follows:

If you should have a lot to say
Just tell it in the simplest way.
Just make it clear and true and terse
And wrap it in a rhyme or verse.

ACKNOWLEDGMENTS

Thanks to the following for their comments on reading the manuscript:

Christine Moroni, publisher
Fran Silverberg, secretary
Dorothy Prelesnik, sister
Veda Ponikvar, proofreader
David Lanari, photo processor
Some priest friends
Chuck Morello's production at IRIS Enterprises

Thanks to Shirley for permission to use her name and photograph in this book. Her comment on reading the script: "That's the way it was."

And, above all, I thank God, the giver of life and love, and ask his blessing on all who read this book.

– Rudy Pakiz

PART ONE

During my more than eighty years of life I have been blessed with fairly good health of mind and body. I enjoyed outdoor physical exercise which included landscaping, gardening and cutting down dead trees for firewood.

At our graduation from the minor seminary some of us celebrated by smoking a cigar for the first time. Just a little puff made me so sick that I never cared to smoke again – except for an occasional magic show in which I made cigarettes disappear. I drank a little wine at socials now and then and loved cold beer on hot summer days but I never became addicted to alcohol, drugs or gambling. Seeing how others ruined their lives by intemperance taught me the importance of moderation.

I was not the brightest student in school and I was deeply aware of my own weakness and vulnerability. I thank God for the guidance of faith which kept me from making more serious mistakes in my life.

Part One of this book is about my search for the meaning and purpose of life. My poor memory does not allow me to describe details or mention all the good people who have influenced me along the way. There are no great accomplishments or outstanding experiences to write about. But I believe the average person can still learn from my thoughts and the path that I traveled.

My own life story came at a time of turbulence in a drastically changing world. How I survived the confusion of a secular culture is the subject of the following pages.

Rudy Pakiz, age 13

CHAPTER I

"Truly you have formed my inmost being;
you knit me in my mother's womb."
Psalms 139/13

The earliest conscious awareness of my existence was when, as a toddler, I would sit on the kitchen floor while the grownups were having dinner. I remember thinking to myself, "Who am I and What am I doing here?" And "Who are these people sitting around the table?"

I soon came to know them as mother, father, brothers and sisters. I didn't fear them as I feared the darkness in the next room. They seemed to tolerate me and, in fact, they took care of me as if they liked me. I guess I could say that they were my "first love".

It was later that I came to understand that each person is unique and is wedded to a particular body distinct from every other individual. Why my soul was assigned to this particular body is still a mystery. Why wasn't I born in Slovenia, Africa or China instead of Minnesota? Was it all a matter of chance or was it Divine Providence? Such were the thoughts that occupied my mind from my earliest years. I was always looking for the answer to the questions "What" and "Why". In a way I was searching for God.

In the New Testament parable of the talents, each servant was asked to take care of some money which was assigned to him by the master. (Matthew 25/14) As human beings we are given a mind, soul and body to take care of and do work with for the glory of God and the good of our neighbors on the planet earth. We are stewards of God's gift of life and we must one day give an account of our stewardship before God.

MY GOD

You loved me before my conception,
regardless of what I might be.
You brought me to life and existence,
and I wonder so often, "Why me?"
You let me experience sorrow
and pleasure and comfort and glee.
You placed me in time on a planet
and promised eternity.

But if there would be no tomorrow,
I'd still want to love You today.
And were there no bliss and no future,
I'd still want to follow Your way.
For with You there is peace and contentment
and in You is "rest," as they say,
So I give You myself as a lover
to do with whatever You may.

Anton and Emma (Zakrajsek) Pakiz

CHAPTER II

"Hear, my son, your father's instruction
and reject not your mother's teaching."
Proverbs 1/8

The love that I had for my mother was a response to her great love for me and my siblings. She toiled and worried and prayed. She often fasted so that the rest of the family might have enough to eat. She baked bread, sewed and mended our clothes. She worked the garden, canned vegetables, fed the cattle, milked the cows and sold the milk, delivered, for six cents a quart.

My mother's hands were worn with toil
that love immersed in suds and soil.

She taught her six children to be frugal, self-sacrificing, trusting in God and grateful for the blessings of life. She walked the children to church which was several miles away from home. She shared with us her faith and what she read about the saints and heroic Slovenian missionaries, like Bishop Baraga and Msgr. Buh.

EMMA ZAKRAJSEK PAKIZ

(1892-1979)

The Springtime of life for mother began
As a home-loving, humble Slovenian.
She was nurtured in faith in a God-fearing home
Where she learned about Jesus and "Thy kingdom come".

The Summer of life brought hardship and toil
As she faced a new life on American soil.
She married and labored to live her new vow.
She brought up her family the best she knew how.

The Autumn of life was beginnings and ends
Of joys and of sorrows among children and friends.
A harvest of peace and a learning to bear
The cross of affliction, of weakness and wear.

For mother the Winter of life has now come
And it brings with it promise of another new home.
May her illness of late be a cleansing and leaven
To bring her the Spring of a new life in heaven. (1978)

My father was not one to demonstrate affection. He was quiet, reserved and somewhat shy but he commanded respect because he wanted what was best for all of us.

ANTON PAKIZ
(1883-1954)

My father led a thoughtful life.
He labored hard and long.
To feed his children and his wife,
to make his family strong.

His humble mien and driving will
inspired his little flock
To work as hard, to sacrifice
and in his footsteps walk.

My father died in 1954 of heart failure at the age of 71. He endured severe pain stoically and never complained to God. I think his Christian faith enabled him to bear it in union with the passion of Jesus.

The reality of suffering and death is still a mystery to me. Perhaps God allows suffering to make death appear to be an escape from this "valley of tears".

And death is not annihilation. It does not wipe out our life's experiences. It does not render useless our acts of love, the good deeds, the thoughts and choices of our earthly life. These we carry with us as our souls go on to a new form of existence.

Justice demands that the wicked be punished and the good rewarded. Otherwise people could "get by with murder" and it would be foolish to sacrifice for the good of others.

Does chance alone explain this?

CHAPTER III

"The fool says in his heart
'There is no God.'"
Psalm 14/1 & Psalm 53/2

As our family began to grow in numbers, our father had to build an upstairs to the house, add electricity and indoor plumbing. With help from the neighbors he enlarged the barn to shelter several cows and a winter's supply of hay. There was plenty of work for everyone in the family and plenty of fun for the children in the neighborhood. We enjoyed playing games, picking berries in the summer and sledding in the winter.

My favorite season was spring – with warm, sunny days and the explosion of life and color and activity. I enjoyed looking for birds' nests, observing insects and marveling at the great profusion of plants and flowers. I knew from childhood that chance alone could not explain the order, complexity and abundance of beauty in nature. Lakes and trees and the great diversity of living creatures filled me with awe and wonder. One of my favorite books was "Wild Animals I have Known" by Ernest Thompson Seton.

It was easy for me to conclude that there must be an Intelligent Being and a Clever Designer behind the animals, the birds and the stars in the sky. I had no trouble believing in God.

It was later that my studies in philosophy and natural science confirmed what I already knew – that there must be an Eternal God, A Necessary Being, one Creator of all those wonderful things. I saw God in the purposefulness of living creatures and the vastness and serenity of the whole universe – an Intelligent Being who not only created all things but continues to sustain them in existence.

THE FIRST CAUSE

Who made the laws that govern time and space
And elements and atoms, bodies, too?
Who put each bone and organ into place
And gave each part a special job to do?
Who made it possible for things to grow,
To move, to blossom, reproduce and heal?
Why can a man remember, think and know
And live and love and reminisce and feel?
What keeps a creature whole – and not apart?
Who made the laws of protons, molecules?
Why is there beauty, harmony and art?
What makes the suns and planets follow rules?
Can chance alone explain a goldenrod?
There is no answer – if there is no God.

Deer resting next to St. Martin's rectory,
Tower, Minnesota

CHAPTER IV

"The Lord's are the earth and its fullness."
Psalm 24

In our family the Church was the center of our social life and the guide to our moral behavior. Love of the Church and love of God were somehow inseparable. It was good to know that other people worshiped in the same church that we did. It was good to see the superintendent of schools and his wife sitting in the front pew of the church during Mass.

I came to understand that going to church was our response to the love of God who made us. By giving us intelligence and free will, God made it possible for us to know Him, love Him freely and thank Him for His goodness.

During my early years the Catholic Church was being attacked in many parts of the world. The Church was outlawed in Mexico and priests, like Fr. Pro, were executed for trying to say Mass in secret. Russia and China were promoting atheistic Communism, and National Socialism became a kind of religion in Europe.

I could not understand how anyone could be an atheist. Logic told me that:

Nothing can come from nothing.

But beings exist.

Therefore there must have been a being that always existed.

And that being is what we call God.

The alternative is to say that the universe always existed. That would mean that the universe was God, which is Pantheism – equating created things with the Creator. I found it easier to believe in a Creator than to imagine creatures somehow being God.

The theory of spontaneous evolution – which says that higher forms of life evolved from chemicals by chance – is a kind of atheism. If living things evolved over the centuries, it must have been by the intervention of the Creator of all things. After all, God must create each human soul at the time of conception and God has power to effect change by grace and through miracles. So there's no reason why He couldn't alter the course of evolution for the survival of species, or have a plan of creation which included change along the way. Chance alone cannot explain how more complex beings can come from simpler forms through spontaneous evolution.

GOD'S ESSENCE

God's essence is just that – "to be",
As Scripture says, "I am Who Am".
God long predated Abraham
By what we call eternity.

Since God existed before time
He is the source of all there is.
All life and energy are His
And all that comes from matter prime.

If things are "good", God must be good.
If there is life, God is the source.
From Him come happiness, of course,
And joy and love and health and food.

G O O D – G O D = O

Nazareth Hall Preparatory Seminary,
St. Paul, Minnesota, 1935

CHAPTER V

"Then I will go in to the altar of God,
the God of my gladness and joy."
Psalm 43/4

The living room in our small home had a pot-bellied stove around which we huddled to keep warm in the cold winter months. The love that we had as a family was like the warmth of that stove that drew us together. But my favorite place was in the kitchen where I watched my mother prepare the meals. The burden of raising a family took its toll on her; she sometimes admitted that she should have gone to the convent.

For me, the warmth of that home was cut short in 1935 when I was 14 years of age. I had completed the 8th grade in the public school and was serving Mass for a Confirmation service. As I was getting ready to go home, the pastor came into the sacristy, looked at me and said, "You, you want to be a priest, don't you? Come and see the bishop." Dumfounded, I stammered that I hadn't thought about that very much. He led me to the rectory and presented me to Bishop Welch. I told him that I couldn't afford to go to the seminary. But the bishop said, "The diocese will pay your way for now." The pastor, Fr. John Schiffrer, then talked to my mother and she agreed to let me go to the preparatory seminary. A few months later I found myself in St. Paul, Minnesota, at a boarding school for boys called Nazareth Hall.

It was nice to meet so many other Catholic boys there and to have priests for teachers. My biggest concern was, "Am I good enough for this kind of life?" My interest in the subjects was adequate but my grades were not the best.

After six years at Nazareth Hall I was sent to the major seminary in St. Paul for studies in philosophy and theology. My hunger for knowledge and a desire to do good sustained me through the decade of schooling away from home. I wanted to learn more; there was no turning back.

The Second World War was raging during those years and I knew we had to defend our country from Japan and Nazi Germany. But I also felt that the Church and the teachings of Christ were the best hope of peace for the world. I continued my studies and prayed for the war to end. The war did end in 1945 and I completed my studies at the seminary a year later. Passing grades were no guarantee of ordination to the priesthood. The real test of a vocation was the official call of the bishop.

In June of 1946 I was ordained a priest for the diocese of Duluth, along with classmates James Crossman and Michael Skumavc.

My first assignments as a priest were in Duluth, Minnesota, at St. James parish and at Holy Rosary Church. St. James was in the west end of the city and had a parochial school. The pastor, Fr. Phillip Kiley, sent his assistants, Fr. George Kryspin and me, to "take census" and in our spare time, plant and harvest beans and potatoes for the school lunch program.

At Holy Rosary Church in east Duluth the pastor, Fr. Joseph Cashin, began to collect money for the new Cathedral to be built on the ledge of rock overlooking the school and Lake Superior. He told the people that the parish appeared to be prosperous enough with a Fr. CASHin and Fr. GOLDen (the other assistant) at the church. Living among the rich and well-educated people of Duluth, I was conscious of my many shortcomings.

Churches were being built throughout the diocese at this time. There were enough priests to take care of them and people seemed to be quite happy with the cessation of hostilities in the world. But the Cold War with the Soviet Union was always on the verge of heating up.

During my early years as a priest I was able to enjoy and develop some hobbies. I learned to do some magic tricks which I used for entertaining children and patients in the hospital, and I joined an amateur magicians' club "for the fun of it." I enjoyed singing with choirs and playing classical music on my stereo record player at the rectory. I enjoyed hunting, hiking, berry picking and bird watching on my days off. I did some oil and acrylic painting but found this hobby very time consuming.

Siblings, 1995:
Mary, Rudy, Dorothy, Victor and Tony
(Genevieve died in 1968)

CHAPTER VI

"I will sing to the Lord all my life;
I will sing praise to my God while I live."
Psalm 104/33

As a priest I visited my folks in Chisholm at least once a month. My life at home with my two brothers and three sisters had been all too brief since I had left home for the prep seminary at the beginning of my ninth grade.

My brothers, Tony and Victor, were drafted and sent to the Pacific Theater during World War II. Tony saw action in New Guinea and vividly remembered the dangers he experienced there. Victor wrote to me about the people and conditions he encountered in India.

Mary worked as a welder in a shipyard in Wisconsin during the War, and for many years, as a clerk in Walgreen's Drug Store in Duluth. She came home to Chisholm to take care of mother who needed special care during her final years. Mary's life was a sacrifice of love. Caring for mother and brother Tony was a duty and a priority for her. She died on Christmas Day in 1998 at the age of 81.

Genevieve worked at a shirt factory and helped with chores around home. She died of cancer at 49 years of age.

GENEVIEVE

They said she had just half a year to live,
My cancer-stricken sister, Genevieve.
What can I do or say? What can I give?
A rose I brought to her one wintry day
For loss of words, to mourn and sympathize.
She didn't smile, she merely turned away
Foreknowing that it also fades and dies.

Dorothy, the youngest of the family, was born in 1933 and did not recognize me as her brother when I came home from school in St. Paul. She married Stanley Prelesnik and had seven children who were a joy to be with, but my visits to see them were infrequent and too short. Separation from home and relatives is not conducive to building solid ties. As the children were growing up, I wrote a few verses about them, such as the following:

DIANE

Diane, you are now at a difficult stage
Not sure what you want in your present teen age.
You're outgrowing the dolls and a bunch of old toys.
You're wondering what's better – horses or boys.

It didn't seem long before the children were all grown up and gone from Chisholm to live their separate lives.

Mission parish at Warba, Minnesota

CHAPTER VII

"As the hind longs for the running waters,
so my soul longs for you, O God."
Psalm 42/2

My first two assignments as pastor were in the rural communities of Floodwood and Carlton. The small town atmosphere was peaceful and friendly. People inspired me with their simple faith and humble life styles. But it was here that I experienced some cold facts of life: a triple murder in my parish, a hunting partner dying in my car and the accidental shooting of a young boy by his brother after I had driven them home from church.

The pastor in a small parish is expected to take care of any kind of problem that comes along. You have to learn to cook for yourself, and sometimes advise visiting hunters where to look for deer. You have to keep the church basement from getting flooded in the spring and see to it that the rectory doesn't burn down from an overheated oil burner in the winter time. You may have to chart a plan for the parish cemetery where the burials have been haphazard in the past. But working outdoors was always a pleasure for me.

One of the reasons I was attracted to the priesthood in the first place was the passage in Matthew 10/29 where Jesus said, "Everyone who has given up home, brothers or sisters, father or mother, wife or children or property for my sake will receive many times as much and inherit everlasting life." I saw some advantages to a celibate life and found the priesthood to be rewarding as well as challenging.

A PRIEST

You leave home and parents
    and God becomes your father and mother.
You leave brothers and sisters
    and gain an endless family in the church
You give up having children of your own
    but there are always youngsters who call you "Father".
You give up worldly wealth
    but have all that you need and more.
You have meager talents and abilities
    but the little you have becomes great.
You hardly know your flock
    but your presence holds the parish together.
You give your all in the process
    but you are promised eternal life.

Jesus set the example for celibacy in the priesthood and called his priests to follow him. For me, the best argument for celibacy was that many people – widows and widowers, the divorced, the single and the disabled – need support and role models for their state of life. Priests and nuns are in a unique position to fill this role, provided they are happy and not breakers of their vows.

In my early life I was strongly attracted to particular girls who were not at all interested in me, and I learned that there were some who liked me but I had no interest in them. At the minor seminary there were "visiting Sundays" on which relatives could come to see the boys at school. I had no visitors because of the distance from my hometown in northern Minnesota, but it was a welcome change to see other people on the campus and in the chapel for Benediction. I was enchanted by the pretty girls that came on such occasions. The prospect of a celibate life did not take away my attraction to girls but the tension made life more interesting.

The priesthood, like any other life, has tensions and temptations. I was to find that out in my next assignment to a popular resort town in central Minnesota at a time when the sexual revolution made great advances and the Second Vatican Council disturbed the "status quo" in the Catholic Church.

St. Martin’s Church, Tower, Minnesota

CHAPTER VIII

"I myself am the bread of life."
John 6/35

The most visible change that occurred after the Second Vatican Council was in the external form of the Mass. The prayers were now said in English instead of Latin and the priest faced the congregation. Though I found it helpful to know some Latin because of its bearing on English words and grammar, I was happy that the Mass could now be said in the vernacular.

The sacrifice of the Mass is the high point for a priest's spiritual life and for a Catholic's worship of God. Scott Hahn, a convert from the Protestant faith, said that the Mass is the closest thing that we have to heaven here on earth.

The sixth chapter of St. John's Gospel is a challenge of faith for the followers of Christ. Jesus said, "My flesh is real food and my blood is real drink. The man who feeds on my flesh and drinks my blood remains in me and I in him." (John 6/55) But "How can He give us His flesh to eat?" (John 6/52)

As a Catholic I believed in the presence of Jesus in Holy communion as the Church understands it but I still wondered why Jesus would institute such a sacrament. With the help of philosophy I came up with the following explanation:

The tendency of love is to be one with the object of affection, whether person, food or anything else. But the closest kind of unity is actually eating the object of our love. We say, "I love you so much I could eat you up."

Jesus loved us so much that He wanted to be one with us. So He came to live among us and then put himself into common forms of food and drink – bread and wine.

But Jesus wanted us to love Him in return and to be one with Him by a free choice. So He invites us to receive Him in Holy Communion. This is the message of the following sonnet:

HOLY COMMUNION

The tendency of love is unity
And two become as one because of love.
Thus, man and woman wed because they see
And want togetherness – like hand in glove.
And when a person eats a piece of pie
The food becomes a part of him or her;
It also helps one grow instead of die.
Perhaps to this does Jesus Christ refer
When, seeking love and unity (the clue)
He puts Himself into the form of food;
"You cannot have the life of God in you
Unless you eat my flesh and drink my blood."
"I love you so much I could eat you up," we say.
To grow in Christ, Communion is the way.

Communion with Jesus, I am convinced, is not only a desirable goal for each individual but the key to the reunion of all Christians which Jesus prayed for in John 17/21 "that they all may be one." Union with Christ is also the sure way to peace among people throughout the world.

My hope in becoming a priest was to help people of other denominations return to the Catholic Church. It was clear to me that the Catholic Church goes back to the time of Christ and that St. Peter and the popes received authority to rule the Church by Jesus himself. The words of Jesus to Peter in Matthew 16/18 cannot be explained away: "You are Peter (rock) and on this rock I will build my church." "I will entrust to you the keys of the kingdom of heaven" (Matthew 16/14) "Feed my lambs, feed my sheep" (John 21/15-18)

Such passages from the Bible show clearly that the authority of Jesus was passed on to St. Peter, the apostles, and to the Popes and bishops of the Church. "And know that I am with you always, until the end of the world." (Matthew 28/20) The Scriptures also show that the Sacraments were commissioned by Jesus to carry on His work. For example, confession: "If you forgive men's sins, they are forgiven them." (John 20/23)

My prayer has always been for unity among Christians so that we may be a greater influence for good in the modern world. It is encouraging to see Protestant ministers becoming Catholic because of their familiarity with the Bible and the writings of the early Church.

I see the Church as a kind of extension of Christ through time and place. Members of the Church are the voice, the hands and the love of Jesus in the world – caring for the sick, educating and uplifting the poor and praising God in churches and homes.

The sacraments are spiritual food for the souls of the faithful who are the branches sustained by the vine which is Christ.

My experience in the priesthood was very rewarding on the whole. There was great satisfaction in helping others in one way or another. But there was also disappointment in seeing the consequences of sin – injuries, murders, suicides and the breakup of marriages. There were converts to the faith and sinners who returned to God, but there were also Catholics who gave up the practice of the faith.

One family inspired me to write this poem:

THE PEW IS EMPTY

The pew is empty, bleak and dull
Where once you sat to worship God.
The air is silent; there's a lull
Where once the feet of children trod.

The house of God is poorer now
With members of the family gone;
With absentees, the test is how
Can fitting praise and thanks be done.

The parish is community
For Christians who believe and hope
And try to follow Christ and be
United with the Church and Pope.

God's kingdom is the Catholic Church
For which the Founder Son was slain.
The shepherd of the flock must search
Till all are safely back again.

Return, then, to the Church that binds
Into one body all who come
With loving hearts and open minds
To find with Jesus Christ a home.

Worshiping God together at Mass is a great support for both clergy and congregation. People of faith can give thanks and praise to God for creatures who are not able to do so themselves. And the very culture of a nation depends on the spiritual life of individuals who assemble in prayer on a weekly basis. This is why attendance at Mass is so necessary.

MISSING MASS

"A"

As usual, I missed Mass today
I had to fish on opening day.
It took me many hours to drive
And with my boat and van arrive
As usual, I missed Mass today.

"B"

Believe me, I missed Mass today.
I was too ill to even pray.
I wish in church I could have been
To thank and praise God once again.
Believe me, I missed Mass today.

St. Paul Seminary Chapel, 1945, St. Paul, Minnesota

CHAPTER IX

"You have made us for yourself, O God,
and our hearts are restless until they rest in you."
– St. Augustine

Our philosophy course at the St. Paul Seminary helped me understand the purpose of life – that God is not only the First Cause and Necessary Being or Creator but also the end or goal of our human existence. Human beings are made to know, love and serve God in this world and to be happy with God forever in heaven.

With our minds we seek All Truth
With our wills we seek All Good

But this world is finite, so we can attain only limited knowledge and limited goods with our limited abilities. What we really desire is to know God who is infinite Truth and to love God who is infinite Good. The attainment of these goals is Heaven. We crave Eternal Life, Astounding Beauty and Enduring Love. All these attributes are to be found in the unity and simplicity of the One God of Christianity.

Our course in Sacred Scripture told of ancient people's belief in monotheism and the coming of God to live among us. Our study of History showed the spread of civilization and Christianity down through the centuries. The major courses were Moral and

Dogmatic Theology but we also studied science and other subjects needed for practical ministry in the priesthood.

In human nature there is a desire for community, power, mobility and forgiveness. In God there is the Trinity of Persons, Omnipotence, Omnipresence and Mercy. As Scripture says, we are made in the image and likeness of God. God is within us and beyond us – He is immanent and transcendent. We go to God through Jesus Christ, the God-Man who founded the Catholic Church.

THE DEEPEST LONGING

The deepest longing of our human soul
Is for a blissful life that never ends,
Complete possession of a perfect goal
With loving people, relatives and friends,
Relieved of imperfections, sin and woe,
Surpassing joys of nature, music, art,
Beyond the limits of delights we know
Or dream of with our searching mind and heart.
That goal is total knowledge, perfect peace,
Enduring beauty, everlasting love,
Ecstatic happiness without surcease,
Unparalleled on earth or sky above.
Our longing is to be with God alone
Whose Life and Love and Beauty are all one.

Although I felt unworthy of guiding souls to eternal life I was convinced that the Catholic Church was instituted by Jesus Christ and was the key to unity among Christians and the only hope for a messed-up world.

Some books which influenced my thinking and my journey in faith, outside of our seminary textbooks, were: "Man the Unknown" by Alexis Carel, the "Confessions" of St. Augustine, "Orthodoxy" by G. K. Chesterton, "Radio Replies" by Fathers Rumble and Carty and "Rebuilding of a Lost Faith" by John Stoddard. In more recent times, my faith has been enriched by the works of Fr. William Carr, Scott Hahn and Mother Angelica's EWTN.

Feeding deer by hand at St. Martin's parish rectory

CHAPTER X

"My son, use freely whatever you have
and enjoy it as best you can."
Sirach 13/11

The Scriptures teach us to "love God above all things and to love our neighbors as ourselves." This is the key message of the Catholic faith and it is a positive way of looking at the Ten Commandments.

During a summer vacation from the seminary I took a job as a counselor at a boys' camp near Brainerd, Minnesota, where the motto was "God is first; others are second; I am third." Sometimes I thought that this was not quite accurate because we are to love our neighbor as ourselves. You can't love others if you do not love yourself. But, of course, all three must go hand in hand: Love of God, Self and Neighbor.

In addition to these basic loves, are the simple loves that occupy our attention, time and energy every day. These include our love for food, recreation, pets and hobbies. Hobbies and pets have been a source of joy in my life and have provided me with diversion, entertainment and useful activity. I don't know how anyone can go through life without such distractions.

Outdoor recreation was an important part of my life. This included hiking, berry picking, hunting, camping, bird watching, gardening, etc. When snowmobiling became popular, I worked with a priest friend and neighbor, Fr. Ed Nistler, in clearing and mapping trails around Walker, Minnesota.

Along with love of nature I enjoyed photography to capture some beautiful scenes in northern Minnesota's lake country. At my present parish in Tower, Minnesota, I did some landscaping around the church and sketched some scenes which were used as a basis for the stained glass windows at St. Martin's Church.

My interest in poetry developed when I found myself correcting or trying to improve upon some of the poems and songs of well-known writers and composers. I enjoyed good music in church and regularly had to lead the congregational singing at Mass. A hobby can be useful as well as enjoyable.

Along with hobbies I had a couple of cats as pets and, more recently, a number of deer that came to my yard for corn in the winter time. Some of them trusted me enough to eat out of my hand.

MY DEER

Your fear of humans, hungry wolves and bear
Keeps you away from what can hurt or kill.
But when the snow is deep, your meals are rare,
Your hunger comes in conflict with your will.

You come for corn and for a better view
To check the tray, then sidle up to me
With faith that I will do no harm to you.
The corn you eat, from fear you are now free.

You bring me joy when you eat from my hand.
It's nice to know that you are still alive.
My love for you I think you understand.
My wish for you is that you all survive.

God is the Source and Terminus of Life and Love

CHAPTER XI

"Is not man's life on earth a drudgery?"
Job 7/1

One day, as a youngster, I took a walk to see the nest of a Cedar Waxwing not far from home. What I found was a dead mother bird with her wings fanned out to protect her little ones who had also died. There was a hole in the mother's skull which was obviously made by a hail storm the previous week. I came home sad on that cloudy day realizing that we are living in an imperfect world.

The same laws of nature that control gravity, combustion and vegetable growth can also cause suffering and death to living creatures. Species of animals, insects and plants are at war with one another for territory, propagation and survival. Among human beings there is sickness, injury and old age, along with miracles of health and new life. Furthermore, there is the evil of sin which causes sorrow, pain and distrust among people. The world seems to be a mixture of good and evil. Water and sun are essential to life but they can also be the cause of death.

Some of the apparent evils, like death, should be seen in the perspective of eternal life where "Eye has not seen, ear has not heard, nor has it so much as dawned on man what God has prepared for those who love him." (I Corinthians 2/9)

Early in life I was aware of sins that threatened the order and well-being of society. I myself was sexually molested by the principal of the Junior High School just before I was to enter the seminary. Ironically, that was a further incentive for me to pursue my studies in moral theology. Scandals were not talked about openly in those days but, as Christians, we were supposed to forgive the sinner and forget the crime.

The prevalence of sin was the most frustrating aspect of my priestly life, but the occasional conversion of a person from serious sin brought joy and encouragement for me, as well as for God. "There will be the same kind of joy before the angels of God over one repentant sinner." (Luke 15/10)

In the struggle between good and evil there is the ideal of Jesus Christ who asks people to follow Him. Then there are the world, the flesh and the devil that tempt us to selfishness, instant pleasure and worldly glory. There is a kind of joy in taking up one's cross daily and trying to be right with God. There is comfort in knowing that suffering has a purpose in God's eternal plan.

I have always had a desire to try to find out the meaning and purpose of life. People seemed to be like cattle – eating and drinking each day to survive, hustling around to raise a family perhaps, and striving to be healthy or wealthy. But for what purpose? To enjoy brief moments of pleasure? To live as long as possible? To what end?

Young people in particular seemed to be searching for some kind of heaven on earth but often ended up like insects caught in a fatal web.

AMOUR

Pleasure seeking, restless boys
unbridled, often go
In search of lonely, careless girls
for whom there is no "No".

Enchanted, tempted, worldly girls
entrapped by blind amour
At last give birth to little ones
not knowing what they're for.

Unwanted children, growing up
deprived of love and joys
Become, in turn, the lonely girls
and restless, worldly boys

The Lord of Christians, called "The Way",
"The Truth", "The Life", "The Door",
Has called them to more wholesome love
and taught them what they're for.

There are powerful instincts in our human nature for our self-preservation and for the preservation of the human species. These instincts can result in ecstatic personal delight and have served the purpose of "filling the earth" with people. But when those instincts are not controlled by reason, self-denial and temperance, they can cause suffering, violence and much unhappiness. History shows what harm can be done by lust for power and personal pleasure. H. W. Crocker, for example, said that England was lost to the Catholic Church because of lust. (Triumph of the Catholic Church)

The sexual revolution of recent years, by liberating society from reasonable restraints, has caused an explosion of pornography, adultery, divorce, cohabitation, contraception and abortion. Unfortunately, the Church itself was somewhat infected by the rebellion.

There are times of darkness when the sun is obscured by the clouds. There are times of pain when the body cannot function as it should. There are times of sorrow and disappointment when God seems far away. There is sadness and frustration because of the evil and violence in a troubled world.

The problem of evil can be partly explained by 1) laws of nature which are basically good for creation as a whole but can cause physical harm to individuals; 2) the sinfulness of people throughout the history of the human race; and 3) the ignorance and errors of people which cause unnecessary conflict and hatred.

A man I knew who was dying of cancer was reluctant to give up his women friends and defended himself by sharing with me the following rhyme:

> King David and King Solomon lived merry, merry lives,
> With many, many girl friends and many, many wives.
> But when old age caught up with them,
> With all its aches and qualms,
> King Solomon wrote the Proverbs
> And David wrote the Psalms.

Unfortunately the man seemed unable to give up his addiction and repent, as David did.

Some of the evils in this world can be prevented by faith, by education and by Christian charity and forgiveness. War and retaliation are not the solution.

WAR

How can a human being speak of war
As any way of generating peace?
No! There can be no compensation for
The injury and harm that wars release.
Revenge and greed and pride and recklessness
Becloud the reason, falsify the goals;
And statesmen, moved by hate and mindlessness,
Remove themselves from death and grieving souls.
With hardened hearts they sacrifice their pawns,
Good men. (Like wood they're cast into the flame)
That no side "wins" for them it never dawns.
Destruction, maiming, doom are but a game.
How can the mighty rulers fail to see
That war is brutalized insanity?

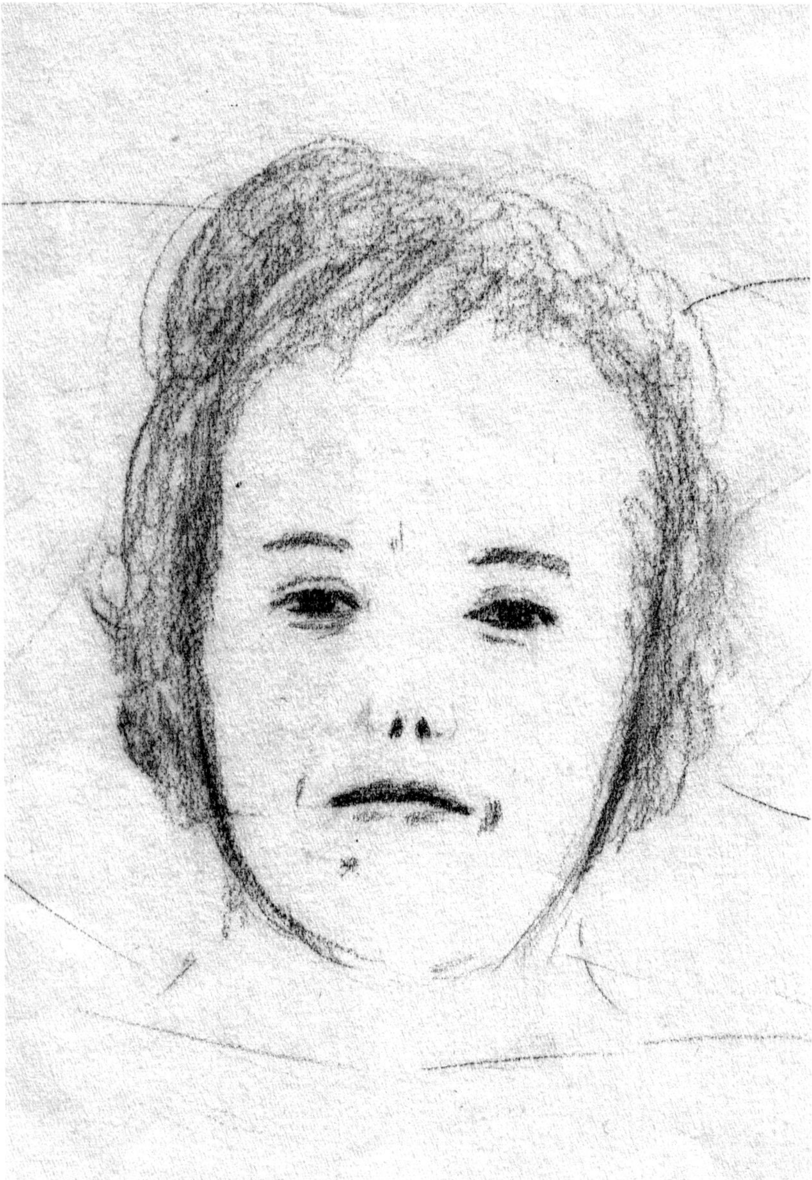

Shirley in the hospital (Sketch by R. Pakiz)

CHAPTER XII

"Deep waters cannot quench love,
nor floods sweep it away"
Songs 8/7

The Second Vatican council was held in Rome in the early 1960s and dealt with many issues concerning the Church in the modern world. Before the documents were published, however, some journalists and periti (advisors to the bishops) gave their own views on what would be decided. There was confusion and uncertainty about the Liturgy and what was to be changed in religious education.

It was reported broadly that the law of celibacy for priests was likely to be changed. This period of confusion resulted in some priests leaving the priesthood and getting married.

It was in this setting that I experienced the crisis of my life. Just as many priests were questioning their own religious vows after Vatican II, I was wondering if I would want to marry if the law of celibacy was to be changed. I had no intention of abandoning my vows but the speculation was intriguing.

One day I drove a carload of parish ladies to a Council of Catholic Women's meeting and on the way back had a car accident. My station wagon was sideswiped by a vehicle that tried to pass as I was turning into the driveway of a passenger's home. When the collision occurred, this passenger fainted and was taken to the hospital. Shirley was kept there for observation overnight.

When I went to see her the next day, she had recovered and there was no visible injury. But, as I tried to speak with her, she reached out to me, kissed me and said, "I love you." She said that she had fainted because she thought I had been injured in the accident. I was flabbergasted! I had always considered her very attractive and talented. She had invited me to dinner at her home a couple of times and I got along well with her husband and their two adopted children. But after the accident she admitted that her feeling for her husband was negative and that she had already been planning a separation. She had married him in the first place on a rebound because her mother was opposed to her previous engagement to a non-Catholic. She thought, perhaps correctly, that her marriage could be annulled by the Church.

For me, to think that the person I most admired really cared for me was an emotional shock. I couldn't think of a more beautiful and charming person to be with. My esteem for her bordered on reverence. We had already become a "mutual admiration society" and, after the accident, she began to visit me and call me on the phone repeatedly. I couldn't forget the day I visited her in the hospital:

SURPRISED BY LOVE

She reached her arm to draw my head against her moistened
cheek.
I didn't know how to react; I simply couldn't speak
She told, forthright, in whispered words the love she had for me.
And then I said, "I love you, too." It came spontaneously.

At once I felt the joy of love, confusion and surprise
That I had been the cause of tears and longing in her eyes.
How could I give her sympathy and not become involved
In her apparent need for love which marriage had not solved.

When there was no news from the Vatican about a change in the law of celibacy, I realized that I was in a dilemma. Providentially, I got a chance to become the pastor in another parish and reluctantly accepted the call. Leaving that parish was an emotional experience; Shirley and I broke down and cried. I moved to the new parish but the wounds healed very slowly. I came to know what it was like to fall in love and have to part. They say it is better to have loved and lost than never to have loved at all. I know now what it means to have a "broken heart".

The cold fact of the matter was that I still had a vow of celibacy to keep and Shirley was still married in the eyes of the Church. Solemn commitments are meant to be honored "till the end of our days". We both had promised to keep.

Shirley

CHAPTER XIII

"How loving and how wondrous fair
must He be who fashioned her."
Coventry Patmore

My English teacher in the minor seminary didn't think much of my poetry so I almost gave up trying to write. But after my encounter with Shirley my interest in poetry revived. When I tried to describe her, the words came out in a rhyme.

ADMIRATION

You're able and remarkable
Artistic and vivacious.
Uncanny and incredible
Executive audacious.

Fantastic and perfectionist
Efficient, cool and winsome.
Most beautiful and kindest,
Superlative and then some.

After the accident I got a short note from Shirley, delivered by her adopted son, Tim. "I am so sorry for the sorrow I brought on you at the time of the accident. Do forgive me, Father." My reply was:

CHRISTIAN LOVE

I have no messenger like Tim to bring my note to you.
I have no one who knows or cares when I am feeling blue.
But when you beg me to "forgive" when I should beg from you,
I know you feel and understand the fears that I went through.
And when you "thank" me, as you say, when I have injured you
I know that there is Christian love that's genuine and true.
The day that you'll be well again, so happy and so gay,
For me that day and not till then – will be Thanksgiving Day.

I had no plans to celebrate my 25th anniversary as a priest but Shirley made the arrangements, put together a photo album and took care of all the details. My life continued to be a mixture of confusion and resignation.

If I cannot love you completely and free
I might as well stick with this celibacy.

If you try to obey both your heart and your head
The result is a lump in your throat instead.

HEARTACHES

From heartaches I look up above
To the sky and the clouds as they move.
But a man finding rhymes
In these troublesome times?
Good heavens! I must be in love.

I was in the middle of a struggle between love of God and love of one of His creatures. The ecstacy of human love was giving way to the reality of life. I had to move on. So when the opportunity came to move to a new parish, I knew that was the will of God. It was not easy but a practical necessity. Shirley had somehow helped me to see that God was my greatest Love.

LOVE IN PERSPECTIVE

You taught me what it's like to be in love,
To feel the high, to see the drab world part.
Your eyes reflected magic from above
Or was it longing from a lonely heart?
While I admired your skills, your charm and grace,
A Providence or Fate ordained that we
Should meet in admiration, time and place.
But reason told me that this shouldn't be –
That we had prior vows, and higher dues
To God, to Church, to work and family.
The thought of parting was "to have the blues".
I moved away, heart broken, torn, asea.
But now I know how awesome love can be.

Let the little children come to me

CHAPTER XIV

"How great are your works, O Lord!
How very deep are your thoughts."
Psalm 92/6

Moving to another parish did not take away the feeling I had for Shirley but communication with her became more impractical. The notes we exchanged were like dying embers – an occasional spark that persisted despite the cold reality of the situation. Like the day she called me on the phone, I wrote to her:

Congratulations! You're the first
to call and quench my thirst
for the sound of a voice on a gloomy day.
Now, aren't you glad that you called today?

And for Shirley's birthday I wrote this note:

My prayer is for joy in whatever you do –
For happiness, peace and a constant plea
That the nicest things will happen to you
'Cause you're the nicest thing that has happened to me.

From knowing Shirley I learned that a Platonic friendship is still possible in a world of cynicism and self-gratification. I have seen friends leave the priesthood to get married without considering an alternative. I learned of divorces and second marriages that could have been prevented if the people had tempered their emotions with love of God. Time and separation can help to cool romances. Knowing that God's will is for the good of society can be helpful. Love of God must supercede the love of any creature, no matter how attractive that creature may be. Finding satisfaction in work and in hobbies can bring contentment and joy. Being right with God is essential.

GOD, HOLD ME BACK

God, hold me back from doing wrong
And push me on to doing good
So that my days be full and long
In doing all I can and should.

Working in a different parish gave me a chance to see new faces and meet new friends, young and old. I had always been fond of children who were filled with the exuberance of life and exemplified the miracle of creation. Now they came to my rectory for games of checkers, chess and table tennis. On hot summer days I would drive them to the lake for an afternoon swim. Jesus had said, "Let the little children come to me, and do not hinder them, for of such is the kingdom of God." (Luke 18/16) Children made me feel young and I enjoyed their company. But that was all to change.

The clergy sex scandals at the turn of the century altered the relationship between priests and young people. Clergy are now supposed to avoid familiarity with children.

I believe that part of the problem with the clergy scandals was that the sexual revolution which began in the 1960s had infiltrated the Church as well as the culture of the day. Liberals attempted to overthrow the basic institutions of society – marriage, the family and the Church. Sex was supposed to be enjoyed by all. Guests of TV talk shows bragged about their sexual exploits. Spontaneous evolution was accepted as a fact, emphasizing our basic animal instincts. Bonobo chimpanzees that indulged in uninhibited sexual activity but lived at peace with one another were portrayed as models for the human race. Cohabitation, adultery, fornication and promiscuous behavior required the invention of the birth control pill. With the failure of contraceptives, abortion was deemed necessary and made legal. No-fault divorces increased and homosexuals demanded marriage rights.

In this culture of death the Church continued to be the defender of life and of the family. But now it was necessary to convert Catholics from pagan ways and attitudes. There was ever more work for parish priests while the number of vocations was declining.

In Thanksgiving

for 50 years in the Priesthood

1946 — 1996

FR. RUDOLPH PAKIZ

"Thanks be to God for
his indescribable gift."
2 Cor. 9/15

OF003
LITHO IN U.S.A. *Symbolic* *Barton-Cotton, Inc.*

CHAPTER XV

"My being proclaims the greatness of the Lord."
Luke 1/46

As I look back on the 83 years of my life I can say that I loved and enjoyed many good things and many good people in a number of parishes in northern Minnesota. But the greatest love of my life, in reality, has been love of God.

There was, first of all, the indelible love of my immediate family and all that we had to suffer and enjoy together. There were classmates in grade school and good teachers who dedicated their lives for our benefit. The preparatory seminary was a beautiful setting to spend my teenage years. I loved my fellow seminarians and the monastic life of the seminary, and the special opportunities to ponder the mysteries of life.

I am grateful to my seminary class for the support and good example they gave me. The priests of the Diocese of Duluth have been an inspiration to me as well. I am grateful for the kindness of people in the parishes in which I worked.

My life spanned most of the 20th century, from the time that groceries were delivered to our homes by horse and wagon, to the age of computerized checkout facilities; from small airplanes to amazing space craft and technology; from steam engines to nuclear power plants; and from crystal sets to digital television.

At the same time, the world witnessed unbelievable destruction and loss of life in major wars, in the annihilation of people in the Soviet Union, Nazi Germany, Cambodia, in Africa, the Holocaust and elsewhere. Many millions died of AIDS, abortion and the misuse of drugs in our "culture of death". The attack on our country by Muslim terrorists has humbled America as a nation and has made us aware of the need for more love and understanding among all the people of the world.

The current struggle of the Catholic Church is about regaining respect and credibility, and about being the people that Jesus wants us to be. The battle is still between the love of God and the love of his creatures. The love of God must always be a first.

WITH EYES OF FAITH

All those who see with eyes of faith
The Beauty of the earth
Can savor all the blessings that
The Lord bestows from birth.

For those who strive wholeheartedly
To love God and obey,
There's peace of mind and joy of heart
And hope on life's highway.

Forbid us, Lord, to ever stray
From your true Church and Way.
Confirm our love and unity
To grow with you each day.

Let's praise the Lord with gratitude;
    Rejoice and never fear.
The God who knows our deeds and thoughts
    Is always very near.

Let all who seek the Lord and God
    Through Jesus Christ his Son
Have grace to rise as Jesus did
    When this brief life is done.

PART TWO

This section is an anthology of my poetry, sonnets, odes and other verses. “Tenting in the Storm,” for example, is an attempt at onomatopoeia, which is using words to mimic the sounds of the action that is described.

I have a preference for poetry that has “rhyme and reason”. As I said in my “Simple Rhymes” booklet, poetry is an expression of thought or deep feeling in a concise format, with descriptive words and rhythmic phrases. It should be understandable, thought-provoking and easy to read or recite. That is still my understanding of poetry, as opposed to prose.

Most people are poets at heart and many enjoy playing with words, such as in crossword puzzles. I think poetry is “playing with words.” I hope that this book will encourage others to write poetry and record their thoughts and aspirations in simple verses for the world to enjoy.

WHEN YOU'RE 60 YEARS OLD

When you're 60 years old you have to admit
That the world keeps on spinning but you'll have to quit.
You can't help but notice again and again
That people your age look so aged – and then
You notice how wrinkled you are – and how gray,
How tired you are at the end of the day.
You go to your doctor. He stops to reflect:
"At your age, of course, what can you expect?"

You feel a lot younger with children around.
They're noisy, they're carefree, with life they abound.
(The young ones say "grandpa"; they visit me still.
The teenagers think that I'm over the hill.)
At 60 you're wise but what good does it do?
The ones who could profit don't listen to you.
You've lived through depressions, recessions and war.
You've learned to accept whatever's in store.

The industrial age has surrendered its place.
To the age of the atom and the new age of space.
The old "Church Triumphal" has now given way
To the new "Church Ignored" in our secular day.
The culture has drifted from left and from right;
It is losing its Christian ideals in the plight.
The energy crisis has let it be known
That life on our planet depends on the sun.

In the past 60 years we have gone very far
From the old horse-drawn wagon to the imported car,
From the kerosene lamp to the electric light,
From the trans-ocean ship to the inter-space flight,
From the telegraph code to the computered fee,
From the crystal set to color TV.
I have witnessed the changes with hopes and with fears.
It was great to be part of the last 60 years.

THANKSGIVING

I thank you, Lord, for my friends and neighbors,
      Family, relatives, distant and near.
I thank you for life and strength in my labors,
      For joy in success and comfort in fear.

I thank you, Lord, for the world you've given
      With beautiful birds and flowers and deer.
I thank you, Lord, for a place in heaven -
      But I really don't mind what I have down here.

BEING A PRIEST (1996)

Being a priest for 50 odd years
Has nothing to do with virtue or brains –
Just keeping your health and outliving your peers
And staying indoors when it snows or it rains.

The Iron Man, Chisholm, Minesota

MESABI'S IRON MAN

To Minnesota's Iron Range
came Finns and Scandinavians,
Italians, Serbs and Greeks and Poles,
Croatians and Slovenians.

To settle in the promised land
to work the mines for iron ore,
To get away from troubled spots
some time before the First World War

They came prepared for heavy toil;
to build a future was their plan.
They worked together hand in hand
and formed Mesabi's IRON MAN:

Fatigued and stooped beyond your years
you work in wretched cold and heat.
The furrows of your ruddy brow
are dark with ochry dirt and sweat.

Your heavy clothes are brown with dust;
your hard hat, like a helmet, crowned
With carbide lamp to light the dark
and eerie caverns in the ground.

There shafts and tunnels pierce the earth
in cold and gloomy passageways
Where small rail cars and cedar ties
assist the miners in the maze.

Your heavy shoes with hardened toes
are reddish brown and worn and bruised.
Your pick and shovel, basic tools,
are ever present and well used.

Determined are your inner powers,
begot of pride and need and will,
To wrench from solid earth the ore
with all your energy and skill.

You think of wife and family,
of food and shelter that they need.
You think of bills, of illness, school.
You want your kids to learn to read –

That they may find a better way
to spend their lives and find success
Without your drudgery and pain,
with comfort, joy and happiness.

You lean on friends and kin to help
you solve your problems day by day.
You lean on faith to give you light
and strength and hope along the way.

You like to drink and dance and play
the accordion and sing along.
And feast and celebrate with friends.
You love the home where you belong.

You supplement your meager wage
with keeping cows for milk and meat.
Your extra energy and time
you spend on cutting wood for heat.

You like to hunt and fish and trap.
You like to pick the berries, blue.
As well as mushrooms in the field.
Your garden is a bonus, too.

Your lunch pail holds the coffee, first,
then pork chops, egg and home-made bread,
Or Polish sausage, apple pie
and cheese, or sandwiches, instead.

Your town is built around the school
and churches where the people go
To celebrate their simple lives
and homage to their Maker do.

Your home is shelter from the cold,
a place for cleaning up and rest,
A shrine for what is good in life
and, for the children, cozy nest.

Your contribution to the world
is mining ore for iron and steel.
Your impact on the lives of all
is indisputable and real.

The Iron Miner has been changed.
His simple tools are minimized,
Replaced by giant trucks and belts
and massive shovels, motorized.

The miners now are more diverse –
mechanics and geologists,
Electric experts and the like
and some computer specialists.

The workers have been unionized;
their wages incomparable
To what the early miner got.
Their life is now more bearable.

But we cannot forget the ones
who worked when mining once began
On Minnesota's Iron Range.
Salute we now the IRON MAN.

A statue of the Iron Man was erected at the entrance to the Ironworld Interpretative Center near Chisholm, Minnesota, on July 4, 1976.

I MIGHT HAVE BEEN

I might have been a Swede or Finn,
    instead of a Slovenian.
I could have been a Turk or Jew,
    a Farrakhan or Donahue.
But God has blessed me from by birth
    above most creatures on the earth,
Made me a priest in His strange plan
    and sent me up to Tower-Soudan.

A FRIEND

You stand by me despite mistakes,
Support me to the end,
Ignore my faults – for goodness sakes –
Believe me, you're a Friend.

SENIOR CITIZENS

The old are shunned and brushed aside as though they're in the
way.
They're often sent to nursing homes where they don't want to
stay.
They may be feeble, blind or lame; their minds are still O.K.
Their bodies may be wearing out, but they have much to say.

The elderly have done their jobs; they tamed the country, vast.
They raised their children, shared and saved and to successors
passed
The legacy, the culture and the monuments which last.
They still have much to give and share – traditions from the past.

The years may take their toll of health; the body may be sore;
The old veneer may hide the gifts, the knowledge and the lore
Which make the senior citizen a veritable store
Of tested wisdom, culled from life as it was lived before.

GOD GAVE ME EYES

God gave me eyes that I might see
the boundless works laid out for me.
God gave me ears that I might hear
the cries for help from far and near.
God gave me hands that I might build
a work of art, see dreams fulfilled.

God blessed me with the power to know
and help someone, somehow to grow.
God blessed me with the power to love
the underdog, and God above.
God gave me freedom that I may
choose what is right and lead the way.

Class Reunion at Gainey House,
Owatonna, Minnesota 1986

CLASS OF 1946

Many started in the fall
          of '35 at Naz'reth Hall.
A smaller number made it through
          the high school years and college, too.

It was a time of growing pains
          for restless boys and active brains;
With priests and nuns to teach and fill
          the hungry bodies, minds and will.

The classrooms, dorms and spacious grounds
          were home for boys, but out of bounds
For girls and other dire temptations
          that might deflect our true vocations.

The St. Paul Seminary years
          were filled with study, prayer and fears
Of how our lives and our Church, too,
          might be destroyed by World War II.

With faith and perseverance strong
          a bunch of us survived the long
Ordeal and were at last ordained
          to serve the Church for which we trained.

There was   Skumavc, Fahnlander
                   Westhoff, Leander
                   Smith and Baumgartner
                   Neudecker, Ginther
                   Roach, Pakiz and Exley
                   Carriere and Dempsey
                   Sobiek, McNulty
                   Schmitzer and Dudley

Schekleton, Murphy
Sebesta and Flatley
Brouchoud and Moorman
Treinen and Shannon
Bonin and Gleason
Simon and Crossman
Lepine and Wittman

With hope and with naivete,
we all went out, each in his way
To change the world and serve the Lord
by holy lives, to preach the Word.

The Latin Mass and all we learned
were soon to be revised, upturned
When John the twenty third decreed
that Church renewal was the need.

The cold war of the great world powers
was balanced by the hot ash showers
Of changes in the Church and strife
of old and new in Christian life.

The conflict had its toll, of course,
but now we look more to the source
Of our vocations and our faith,
our final Goal – and even death.

The world is getting tired of war.
The Church is hanging in, but sore.
Our class has done its level best.
We trust that God will do the rest.

- Mike Skumavc & Rudy Pakiz

SCHOOL WITHOUT GOD

Today we have to go to school
Where praying is against the rule.
In this great nation under God
To mention Him in school is odd.

If Bible verses one relates –
That violates the Bill of Rights.
And if a child in prayer does bow –
That may be more than rules allow.

For praying in a public hall
Might shame those with no faith at all.
In silence one must meditate.
God's name is tabooed by the state.

'Tis fine to curse and dress like freaks,
Have pierc-ed noses, tongues and cheeks;
O.K. that hair be or'nge or green
But criticizing would be mean.

It's fine to choose a pregnant Queen,
An unwed father King and teen.
Beware of teaching right from wrong
For "judgments" there do not belong.

Free sex, condoms and women's pills,
Witchcraft, vampires and wars to kill –
Such lunacies are freely taught.
But Ten Commandments? They are not!

If God cannot be taught in school
Then parents must make it a rule
To teach by word, by prayer and deed
About the God that children need.

- Anonymous teenager, revised by Fr. Pakiz

PROLOGUE TO CLASS DIRECTORY

The hand of providence has joined us in the class of forty six.
We came from families in ways diverse; we were a motley mix.
But faith has joined us in pursuit of truth and knowledge of the
Word,
And gathered us into a group of men enamoured of the Lord.

The hand of providence has scattered us, as priests on midwest
lands,
To offer up our lives and all as messengers of God – and hands.
As half a century now has lapsed we come before the Lord again,
To give ourselves once more to God as weary and yet hopeful
men.

MEMORIES

The years are passing by like flicks on television screens
And memories pile up within with warm but dimming scenes
Of friendship deep and zest for life that filled our youthful years
As well as sadness, loss and pain accompanied by tears;
And, of the memories that glow in clarity and hue
Are thoughts of precious moments bright that once were shared
with you.

JACK ROACH & I

Jack Roach and I began one fall
The prep sem course at Nazareth Hall
We studied there with other youth
He for St. Paul, and I Duluth.

And at the major Sem we, too
Continued on through World War II
Since then Jack rose to national fame
And Catholics all have heard his name.

As scholar Jack did much research.
As bishop he spoke for the Church.
While Rudy tried with scant reserve
His bishop and his flock to serve

While Roach is preaching this retreat
I occupy the front row seat.
Archbishops have a lot to say
But I just listen and obey.

-Retreat at Buffalo, 1998
Archbishop John Roach, Retreat Master

DEBBIE AND GARY

Debbie and Gary deserve a nice wedding.
They planned and they waited for a blessed new life.
They worked and curtailed any foolish carousing.
They prayed to be loyal as husband and wife.

On the 19th of June at six in the evening
At the old Catholic Church in the New Prague town
The groom spoke commitment in a covenant wedding
And the bride did the same in a white wedding gown.

The marriage united two hearts and some others
And lifted their spirits with grace from above.
And that is God's plan for fathers and mothers –
To leaven the earth with new life and new love.

YOU'RE AN IMAGE OF GOD

Blessed are you, the image and likeness of God.

You, child of God, are the mystical moon,
Reflecting the glory of God in the darkness of night.

You, child of God, are a candle's flame,
Lit by the truth of an all-knowing God, so bright.

You, child of God, are a delicate eye,
Filled with the beauty of God, His color and light.

You, child of God, are a wide-open book,
Sharing your thoughts and giving others delight.

You, child of God, are a pillar of strength,
Bearing your burdens with courage and patience and might.

You, child of God, are a beautiful gem,
Reflecting the goodness of God in doing what's right.

You, child of God, are a treasure of art,
Molded in faith and polished by grace in God's sight.

Blessed are you, the image and likeness of God.

GOD'S AUTOMOBILE

The world's most perfect automobile
Has neither brakes nor steering wheel.
It has no metal doors, or glass,
No batteries, no oil or gas.

The frame is made of skull and bone
And muscles tough, and teeth like stone.
The bones comprise a skeleton
That lets the body move and run.

The outer parts are wrapped in skin
To shelter organs safe within
From germs and grit and weather's storm.
Two eyelids keep the eyes from harm.

Within the body as a whole
Are parts that play a special role
To make the total function best –
Each organ working with the rest.

The heart is made to pump the blood
Which to each cell provides some food.
From lungs it brings essential air
From lower parts digested fare.

From outer sense of touch and taste
To final getting rid of waste
The body, like a factory
Accepts, rejects selectively.

The body has its lungs and heart,
Its kidney, liver – each a part.
But there is more than gut or spleen.
There is a soul that can't be seen.

The soul looks out with searching eyes
To see a world of earth and skies,
And with the help of ears and nose
Perceives the trees and birds and rose.

The soul can also look beyond
And with intelligence respond
By praising God by whose design
It first was built – by grace divine.

The soul is driver of the car
Which travels daily near and far.
The soul must care for it as well
To keep it safe from harm and hell.

The Lord entrusts to each of us
A body like a car or bus
So we can drive and safely come
To God's abode – our heavenly home.

EXERCISE

In the first three decades of life, it's true
That exercise livens and strengthens you.

The next three decades require the same
Good use of muscles, mind and frame.

But then the effort of mind and will
Just tires you out as you go downhill.

TENSIONS

"How am I doing?" we so often say
As we seek approval in a worldly way.
We treasure acceptance, conformity
And avoidance of tension to make us free.

But easy surrender is not always good;
The purpose of struggles is misunderstood.
We need to have hungers, conflict and strife
To grow and develop our spiritual life.

Temptations can make us better or worse,
Give us a blessing or bring us a curse.
We must not succumb to the sins of the world
Or fall for the glitter to which we are lured.

Sincere affirmations are good for the soul
As long as they point to our heavenly goal;
But easing the tension with evil or sin
Is losing the battle of life from within.

- Rudy Pakiz, inspired by a talk by Fr. Larry Gillik

RIPPLES

I speak a word. It travels far beyond the place and time of birth.
Its consequences, unforeseen, could ripple on throughout the earth.
Since we can never know the good or evil that our thoughts impart
We must be very sure that what we say is wholesome from the start.

The only one who knows the limits of the influence we share
Is God who, by the ripples of his power, is present everywhere.
So, when we exercise the freedom that we have to love or kill
We better see to it that all conform to His eternal will.

NON-VIOLENCE

Good Lord, you came to bring Good News
to men, to teach, to save and heal.
You came to find the sinners' worth,
to raise him up, your love reveal.
You came to serve, to mend our broken
hearts, to give us hope, relief.
You came to show the way to peace.
You asked for loyalty, belief.

At first the early Christians were
prepared to die for truths like these.
They gave their lives without a fight,
like Christ, with love of enemies.
They lived in peace and persevered
in love for all the world to see
They won the admiration of
the pagans for their loyalty.

But when the first enthusiasm
waned, with persecutions' cease,
The Christians soon forgot your Way,
your radical approach to peace.
They took up arms, with cross on shield,
and sallied forth in needless strife.
For you, O Lord, they now would kill,
despite your reverence for life.

Eight scores of centuries have passed
and wars and violence profused.
The hatreds have mushroomed with time.
Cruel instruments of war are used.
Now Christian people lead the world
in killing and atrocities.
What happened, Lord, to all you said
about the love of enemies?

– Based on talks by Fr. Charles E. McCarthy

JESUS

You're the focal point of history but still the Timeless One.
In spirit you're within us and you're far beyond the sun.

You're silent when we seek you but you once spoke loud and
    clear.
You let us risk our freedom but your help is always near.

You came to raise our spirits, build our hopes, our dreams and
    joy.
You understand our problems, for you once were just a boy.

You taught us not to worry although dangers come with strife.
You promised to your faithful a reward of endless life.

You gave us strength and comfort, though rebellious we be.
You heal us and forgive us if we humbly bend our knee.

HUMILITY

A true perspective shows that God is the
    beginning and the end.
'Tis well to keep this goal in mind
    with spouse, companion or friend.

It's foolish to parade in pride
    with fans, the wealthy and the pearled.
It's tragic to believe you are
    the hub and center of the world.

THE LORD IS EXTRAVAGANT

The Lord is extravagant in His generosity.

He gives more than enough dry weather
so that we can appreciate the rain.
He gives more than enough cold weather
so that we can appreciate the warm.
He gives more than enough friends
so that we can appreciate solitude.
He gives more than enough work
so that we can appreciate relaxation.
He gives more than enough material goods
so that we can appreciate having less.
He gives more than we need
so that we can share with others.
He gives us more than enough suffering
so that we can long for the joys of heaven.

Praised by God in His generosity and extravagance.

OVERWEIGHT?

How can you tell you are overweight?
Is there a number on your scale?
Or constant nagging from your mate?
Or doctor's warning without fail?

The answer is a simple one.
A mirror on the wall will do.
And can you daily jog or run?
Or, simply, can you tie your shoe?

THE GREATEST GOOD

"What is really good?" I ask, "and what's our aim and goal?
And what's the purpose of our life, the object of our soul?"

"Justice" – says the lawyer.
"Knowledge" – says the school.
"Truth" – replies the wise man.
"Pleasure" – says the fool.

"Love" – replies the maiden
"Beauty" – says the bard.
"Treasure" – says the dreamer.
"Safety" – says the guard.

"Fame" – the politician.
"Order" – says the king.
"Money" – says the banker.
"Health" – the people sing.

"Freedom" – says the bondsman.
"Fun" – the circus clown.
"Sex" – the young romantic.
"Peace" – the country town.

"Food" – the heavy glutton.
"Booze" – the imbiber.
"Drugs" – the hapless addict.
"Thrills" – the teen-ager.

Yet none of these can satisfy for any length of time;
But only God, the source of all, eternal and sublime.

O Lord, you made us for yourself. You are all good and true.
Our hearts are restless till they beat in harmony with you.

ARMY WORMS 2000

Recently I waged a war
With pesky army worms galore.
To save my precious apple trees
And all the fruit my mind forsees.

I sprayed the clusters that I found
On trunks of trees where worms abound
In close formation, camouflaged
Till some fell, poisoned and dislodged.

The ones remaining then regrouped
While some, disabled, merely drooped.
The next day more replaced the dead
And some kept dropping on my head.

Just where they came from is a myst'ry
"War is hell" throughout all history.
I still persisted crushing, spraying,
Never winning – just delaying.

More worms came and many scattered,
Killing thousands I am flattered.
But in the end I still see more.
I've won some battles – lost the war.

THE CHICKEN FARMER

The farmer went deep in red
To keep his poor chickens all fed.
So he taught the whole brood
To live without food
And the animals simply dropped dead.

NEW YEAR

Every hour and every minute
Holds a bit of New Year's in it.
And each single one of these
Carries possibilities –
Opportunities for pleasure,
Sharing with someone a treasure,
Making a "Good Morning" cheery,
Comforting the sick and weary,
Making bright the world we live in,
Using all the grace we're given,
Shutting tight the lips to hide
Ugly gossip safe inside,
Healing wounds and building bridges,
Pruning thorns and smoothing ridges.
Let us make a little vow
To come alive beginning now
And, with God's help, to live his way
And make each day a New Year's Day.

- Mary Carolyn Davies & Rudy Pakiz

THE BREATH OF LIFE

The breath of life goes in and out
to nourish and refresh.
It brings in oxygen, clean air,
to vivify the flesh.

The grace of God must be received
before we let it go
To fill the world with light divine
and help us all to grow.

The Eucharist that is our food
we take with open hand
That, once received, we share God's life
and live by his command.

- Based on talk by Fr. Larry Gillick, S.J. 1993

THE PRESENCE OF JESUS

I see His blood upon the crimson rose
And in the stars, the glory of His eyes.
His body gleams amid eternal snows.
His tears fall from the cloudy skies.

I see His face in every gorgeous flower.
The thunder and the singing of the birds
Are but His voice and echoes of His power.
And rocks are firm as are His written words.

- Joseph Plunket & Rudy Pakiz

UNITED CATHOLIC APPEAL RALLY SONG

O give with a smile, a donation worthwhile
When the worker comes up to your door.
For, if you do not part, with enough from your heart
He may have to come back for some more.

I PRAYED

I took some time to think of God.
I groped for words wherewith to speak.
I looked for signs of some response.
I simply prayed.

I didn't really feel or sense.
I didn't find the magic words.
I didn't see the power of God.
I simply prayed.

GOD'S WILL

All Christian folks are taught to pray
"Thy kingdom come, Thy will be done."
But what they often really say
Is "Let me, Lord, have my own way."

ADVENT PRAYER

Lord, give me grace to see the good
In every person, priest and hood.
Give me a sense of humor, too,
That I may come with joy to you
In sorrow for my many sins,
In thanks for my occasional wins,
In adoration on my knees
To ask you favors, if you please,
So that with you I may abide
This advent and this Christmastide.

THE ATHEIST

"You Christians are all hypocrites," said he, the atheist,
"No better than the rest of us, I really do insist.
At least I know there is no hell, and there's no deity.
And when it comes to being good, and to morality,
Thank God, I'm not as bad as you and others I could list.
For me there is no sin, of course, since God does not exist."

YOUTH AND OLD AGE

When we were first born we were helpless and small
And when we grew up we were stronger and tall.
But then in our old age we lose weight again
With wrinkles for women and baldness for men.

As babies we didn't need teeth or much hair.
We depended on mother for food and for care.
As elderly people we again must depend
On others, like children, for a nurse or a friend.

WITH OLD AGE COMES WEAKNESS

With old age come weakness, fatigue and ill health
That tempt one to give up the effort to live.
But beauty and friendships and products of wealth
Can seem more attractive than the alternative.

LOVE

The human heart is made to love
whatever's good and right.
It loves the wise, the talented,
the kind, the brave, the bright.
The human heart cannot but love
the beautiful, the true.
The human heart loves godliness.
Than's why my heart loves you.

FAITH – HOPE – LOVE

Our Faith through the Church we receive.
Our Hope in one God we conceive.
But when we hate others
We don't show our brothers
That Christians in Love do believe.

EASTER

The Spirit of Jesus is with us today,
For He "rose from the dead" as the Scriptures say.

As the real Son of Man He's our king and our Lord.
As the real Son of God He can now be adored.

By His death He is one with all people on earth.
By His rising He gives us a sign of new birth.

He is Hope in a world of suffering and sin.
He is Joy to the faithful who let His grace in.

A DAY AT MABEL LAKE

Morning dawns and birds awake.
Chipmunks stir and robins take
Time to bathe and time to make
Melody at Mabel Lake.

Moles and skink to hiding go.
Bluebirds, finch and vireo
By their songs and beauty show
God is present here below.

Fishing boats in anchor lie.
Pine trees reach up to the sky.
Eagles soar on breezes high.
"Praise the Lord" they seem to cry.

Cool the water, late in June
Spells refreshment for the loon
Warm the sunshine, after noon
Means siesta for the coon.

In the clearing of the land
There's a beach and on the sand
Lazy bathers, slowly tanned,
By the breeze are gently fanned.

Mabel Lake is God's retreat
For the tired and aching feet,
From the desk and busy street,
From the dust and burning heat.

Thirsty deer routinely seek
Water at the lake or creek
Just as Christians every week
Turn to God, as creatures meek.

Near the shore at end of day
Muskrats swim and otters play.
Beavers toil as if to say,
"Rest tomorrow, work today."

With the sunset stillness falls
Broken only by loon calls.
Darkness then the forest palls,
Signaling the hooting owls.

Moonbeams brighten up the night
Turning clouds to silv'ry white.
Lapping waves reflect the light
Saying softly "All is right" -
At Mabel Lake

TENTING IN THE STORM

Alone and awake in my tent by the lake
I reflect on the joys of the day
And the stillness of night, as the fire burns bright,
a symbol of peace and of love.
Mosquitoes, however, outside the tent hover,
like trials along life's way.
The darkness of night is like absence of Light
and the Splendor of God from above.
I ponder like this, as I marvel in bliss
at the wonders of nature around
The tent and the lake and the wavelets that make
such a peaceful, melodious sound:
Splashing the shoreline, splashing the ground.

Mabel Lake, Remer, Minnesota

The moon lights the docks and the clouds and the rocks
        and the lake with a silvery sheen;
But now it is blurred and with dark clouds obscured,
        foreboding an ominous storm.
A breeze comes to life and foreshadows a strife
        in the now darkened wilderness scene.
Then a rumbling behind sheet lightning and wind
        provides obvious warning to form
An ample alarm, to prevent any harm,
        to the creatures that roam in the night.
The wind strains the tent that could likely be rent
        as it shakes with the sound of a kite:
Its canvas aflutter and shutters zipped tight.

Expecting the rain I decide to remain
in the shelter that's staked to the ground,
Surmising the form of the oncoming storm
in my lonely predicament.
I cringe at the clap of the lightning rap
and recoil at the thundering sound.
I prayerfully nod to the mercy of God
and confide in my trustworthy tent;
And I sit through the din with a confident grin
as a gust bends the branches and trees;
And the lightning claps and the canvas flaps
as a gale wind replaces the breeze:
Loud clapping and flapping, whistle and wheeze.

The first drops of rain drop, and splatter and plop
as they pelter the roof of the tent.
With thunder and flashes the rain water splashes
and heavy the torrent descends.
The fire is quenched and the woodland drenched
as the deluge continues unspent.
But the shelter abides, the racket subsides
and the tormented forest unbends.
The fury is crumbling and only a rumbling
persists of the tempest and roar.
The tent has survived, the woods seem revived
and nature is calm as before:
Just a plop, pitter patter, then a patter no more.

Kit meets a stranger

MY KIT

I feared for him the very day they brought him into town.
A city is no place for cats who need to roam and climb
Untethered, and to huddle under brush, not trucks nor cars.
My other cat survived a meager month or so of time
In this domain of creepy cats and roaming, hungry dogs.
A kitten would be doing well if it could reach its prime.

He came to me one Sunday, unexpected and unearned.
Just "Here's a little cat," they said - and how could I refuse?
Its fur was white and shiny black, its white legs long and strong.
The lively kitten fit the bill to charm and to amuse.
He seemed to like my parish house. I loved him from the start.
His youthful and his friendly ways I hoped he'd never lose.

Kit liked to run, to hide and seek, to play with ball and string.
He learned to fetch the candy wrap that seemed to squeak when
found.
He climbed the curtains till he knew that "NO" was not a game.
He peered out from the window to survey the snowy ground.
He longed to romp in fluffy snow and climb the lilac bush
To look for birds, and flee from dogs who often came around.

At night he cuddled up to me for safety and for warmth.
He nudged me gently with his paw, refreshed, at break of day
And led me to the bathroom for his grooming and massage.
He sat up like a dog to beg, but - take a bath? No way!
Philosopher at seven months the kitten tried to see
Where water came from at the sink and why it went away.

At Christmas time he stole the show with kinfolk old and young.
He loved to ride, if not too far, in my new Oldsmobile.
He rode on my toboggan and he soloed down the slide.
He followed me half way to town when I went for the mail.
His greatest fun was in the church. He'd scamper down the aisle.
He'd leap sure-footed o'er the pews and walk the choir loft rail.

The fact that Kit left hairs around the house and clothes and car
Was not his fault; there was no guile, no malice in my pet.
His need to climb and hone his claws was part of what he was.
If human beings wanted to, they all could learn a bit
From Kit: about respect and love (no hate, no spite, no greed).
If everyone would loving be, the world would benefit.

One day my Kit was sitting by the door behind the house.
A child came bolting out just then and struck a mortal blow.
Kit's tender body was no match for sharp-edged metal doors.
He died next day, as mortals do; (some day we all must go).
The modern world is cold and cruel to helpless little cats;
The rabies shots do nothing for the hazards here below.

If I could add a final word to Kit, I'd say to him:
"I thank you, Kit, for what you were: just like a little kid."
The kindest, dearest, truest friend; the best cat I have known.
If you could sit upon my lap as you so often did,
And look at me with searching eyes and eager perked up ears,
I'd tell you how you cheered me up and what your purring said:

That you were happy and content and that you aimed to please;
That you were meant to bring a smile, as now you make me sad.
I thought you were a work of art, made by the hand of God.
You brought a little sunshine in a world of good and bad.
The rectory is quiet now, the unused leash remains.
It was your life you gave to me - the only one you had.

ALLEY

I have a little fluffy toy
that's often at my heels.
It doesn't need a battery
or gas or springs or wheels,
It's soft and warm and cuddly,
to kids it most appeals.
It goes all night and sleeps all day
except for during meals.

This little toy can move and walk
and curl up on a mat.
It purrs when stroked and meows for food;
it's getting pretty fat.
It sneaks about, it's curious,
it's quiet as a bat.
Of course you know of what I write;
he's just an "alley cat".

TWAS THE NIGHT

Twas the night before Christmas
And all through the house
Only me and my cat
And, of course, not a mouse.

TO A CARDINAL

You reign supreme from top of tallest tree.
You wear a crown and coat of majesty.
Your kingdom lies as far as you can see.

The melody you sing is loud and sweet.
How dull the earth without your vocal treat.
How very pleasing is your tweet, tweet, tweet.

Of all the birds you are most bright and gay.
Your crimson red makes warm a wintry day.
Why don't you come more often up our way?

A NATION

There are three things that have to be
To keep a Nation strong and free
One is the home that's bright and dear,
With busy, happy, loved ones near.

One is a ready heart and hand
To love, defend and serve the land.
One is a worn and beaten way
To where the people go and pray.

So long as these are kept alive
A Nation's people will survive.
God keep them always, everywhere,
The Hearth, The Flag, The Place of Prayer.

- Anonymous quotes,
revised by Fr. Rudy Pakiz